Learning from Bad Ideas

BUILDING BLUNDERS

BY AMIE JANE LEAVITT

CONSULTANT:
KATHERINE SOLOMONSON
SCHOOL OF ARCHITECTURE
UNIVERSITY OF MINNESOTA

CAPSTONE PRESS
a capstone imprint

Capstone Captivate is published by Capstone Press,
an imprint of Capstone.
1710 Roe Crest Drive
North Mankato, Minnesota 56003
www.capstonepub.com

Copyright © 2020 by Capstone. All rights reserved.
No part of this publication may be reproduced in whole or in part, or stored in a retrieval system, or transmitted in any form or by any means, electronic, mechanical, photocopying, recording, or otherwise, without written permission of the publisher.

Library of Congress Cataloging-in-Publication Data is available on the Library of Congress website.
ISBN: 978-1-5435-9210-8 (library binding)
ISBN: 978-1-4966-6619-2 (paperback)
ISBN: 978-1-5435-9214-6 (eBook PDF)

Summary: See some of the world's biggest building blunders up close and personal. Find out how each structure failed, the basic building block that was missed during construction, and what engineers learned from their mistakes.

Image Credits
Alamy: Alpha Photo, 34, Keith J Smith, 18, Tracey Whitefoot, 10; Associated Press: 38, Yonhap, 41; Getty Images: Spencer Grant, 14; iStockphoto: stockcam, 8–9; Newscom: Photoshot/UPPA/uppa.co.uk/Band Photo, 42, ZUMA Press/Zhi Jianping, 29, 30; Shutterstock: Aerovista Luchtfotografie, 37, 45 (bottom), blambca, cover (person), Elijah Lovkoff, 21, 45 (top), EQRoy, 22, Fedor Selivanov, 44 (top), IR Stone, 19, JoWen Chao, 17, Marco Rubino, 13, Marnikus, 6, PhotoFires, 5, Tavarius, cover (building), Tupungato, 25, 44 (bottom), voyata, cover (background); Wikimedia: Public Domain, 26, 33, Rolf Gebhardt, 7

Design Elements: Shutterstock

Editorial Credits
Editor: Mari Bolte; Designer: Jennifer Bergstrom; Media Researcher: Eric Gohl; Production Specialist: Laura Manthe

All internet sites appearing in back matter were available and accurate when this book was sent to press.

```
Printed and bound in the United States of America.
PA100
```

TABLE OF CONTENTS

CHAPTER

1 FALLING DOWN
THE LEANING TOWER OF PISA 4

2 TWISTED TOP
CROOKED SPIRE CHURCH 8

3 FALLING GLASS AND SWAYING FLOORS
JOHN HANCOCK TOWER 12

4 THE DEATH RAY
VDARA HOTEL AND SPA 16

5 ALL ANGLES
RAY AND MARIA STATA CENTER AT MIT 20

6 BEND AND SNAP
THE AON CENTER 24

7 LIKE DOMINOES
LOTUS RIVERSIDE 28

8 ON DISPLAY
THE CRYSTAL PALACE 32

9 NO GOAL
GROLSCH VESTE 36

10 NOT-SO-MIGHTY MALL
SAMPOONG DEPARTMENT STORE 40

TIMELINE 44
GLOSSARY 46
READ MORE 47
INTERNET SITES 47
INDEX 48

Words in **bold** are in the glossary.

WHAT GOES UP MUST COME DOWN! It's the most basic concept in the law of gravity, but one every architect hopes to overcome. Unfortunately, a simple mistake can lead to huge building blunders. Learn about these blunders, and think about what can be learned from such massive mistakes.

CHAPTER 1
FALLING DOWN
THE LEANING TOWER OF PISA

Pisa, Italy

FACT: In Greek, *pisa* means "marshy land."

The Leaning Tower of Pisa is located in Tuscany, a region in Italy. It stands near the Tyrrhenian Sea. Its builders didn't mean for it to be famous, though. The tower is known for one thing—its lean.

Construction on this circular bell tower began on August 9, 1173. However, the land in Pisa really wasn't suitable for a tall, heavy marble structure. The ground is marshy and made up of clay, sand, and shells. By the time the builders had completed the third story, it was obvious that there was going to be a problem. The structure had already started tilting to one side as the soil underneath began to shift and settle.

Engineers searched for a way to straighten things out. But a war stopped their work. Nobody touched the tower again until 1272.

By this time, the tower was tipping even more. Builders added extra stone to the shorter side to correct it. This didn't make the building stand up straight, though. Instead, it made the upper floors lean in the opposite direction and gave the building a slight banana shape.

In the end, all seven floors were built without the bell tower falling over. Engineers today still marvel that the builders were able to achieve this. The final floor, which houses the tower's bells, was finally completed in 1399.

When the tower was built, Pisa was a port city.

Over the centuries, the tower has continued to lean to the south. Efforts to stop the lean just made things worse. By 1990, the tower was leaning around 5.5 degrees. Computer models had predicted that the tower would collapse at 5.4 degrees. Fortunately, the models were wrong.

RESTORATION WORK

In 1990, the tower was closed to the public for safety reasons. Engineers came up with a way to **stabilize** the tower. They removed soil from the north side and added weights to the tower. With this plan, the tower was literally pulled back up. Work was completed in 2001. With its tilt now at 3.99 degrees, the tower reopened for tours.

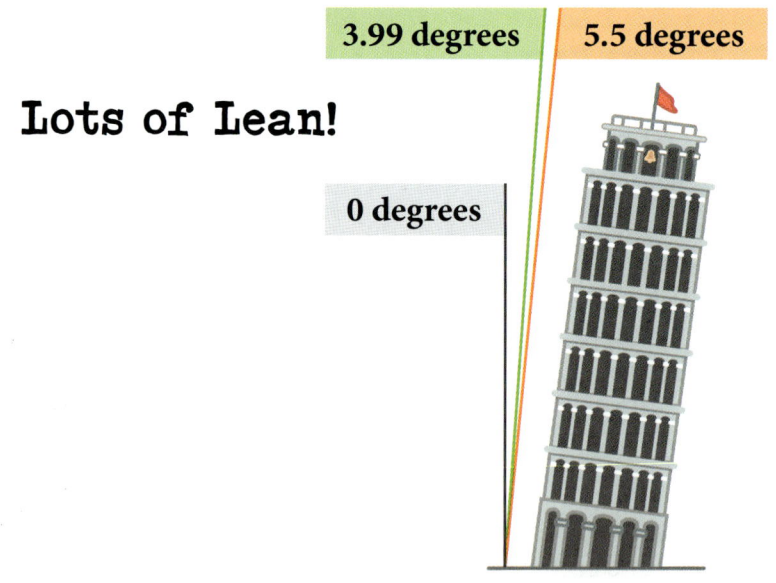

Lots of Lean!

In 1990, lead counterweights were placed at the base of the tower on the north side.

Lessons Learned

Engineers need to study the soil content in an area to make sure it is stable for the type of structures they want to build. If not, a leaning tower could be the least of their worries. Buildings built on unstable surfaces often completely collapse, slide, or topple over.

CHAPTER 2
TWISTED TOP
CROOKED SPIRE CHURCH

Chesterfield, England

St. Mary and All Saints Church is also known as the Crooked **Spire** Church. It is located in Chesterfield, a large market town in England.

The church was built in the late 1200s out of stone that was local to the area. A grand spire made of wood was added around 1360. Its twisted top looks like something that belongs in a fairy tale. But its builders didn't intend for the spire to turn out this way.

Many **superstitious** people in medieval Europe feared that it was a bad sign when the spire twisted. In reality, though, the twisted spire has nothing to do with good or evil. It has everything to do with science.

The church spire is about 228 feet (70 meters) high.

SCIENCE, NOT SUPERSTITION

Experts believe that the spiral shape likely occurred because the builders used green wood to build the spire. Then, to add to the problem, they covered it with green wood shingles and heavy lead roof tiles. As the green timber dried, it shrank and **warped**. The weight of the lead caused the spire to twist. Experts also think that the spiral happened because the builders did not add proper **bracing** to the **superstructure**.

The lead shingles covering the spire weigh 32 tons (29 metric tons).

Green Wood

Wood from trees that have recently been cut is called green wood. Trees, and therefore green wood, are full of moisture. As green wood dries it shrinks.

It takes a special process to properly **cure** wood so that it's ready to use in construction projects. The wood has to be stacked horizontally. Then it is placed under pressure. This helps it air-dry flat and level, without warping. It can take years to dry wood this way. Another technique to get a similar result uses a special oven. But if uncured green wood is used, the final product will end up twisted, warped, and spiraled.

Lessons Learned

Construction workers must use properly prepared materials on a project or nature will take its course. They also must use proper bracing to support a structure. Without bracing, buildings will fall victim to natural forces.

CHAPTER 3
FALLING GLASS AND SWAYING FLOORS
JOHN HANCOCK TOWER

Boston, Massachusetts

The John Hancock Tower is a 60-story skyscraper. Though it is Boston's tallest structure—and a famous landmark—it almost became a building blunder. And it was all because of the wind.

Construction started in 1968. The designers wanted the 790-foot (240-meter)-tall tower to sparkle. They covered the outside with more than 10,000 shining panes of glass that cost $700 each. The city's historic buildings reflected off the glossy blue glass. On clear days, the reflection of the blue sky made the building look almost invisible.

There was one problem, though. Every time the wind blew faster than 45 miles (72 kilometers) per hour, glass panes would pop off the building. They would crash hundreds of feet onto the streets below.

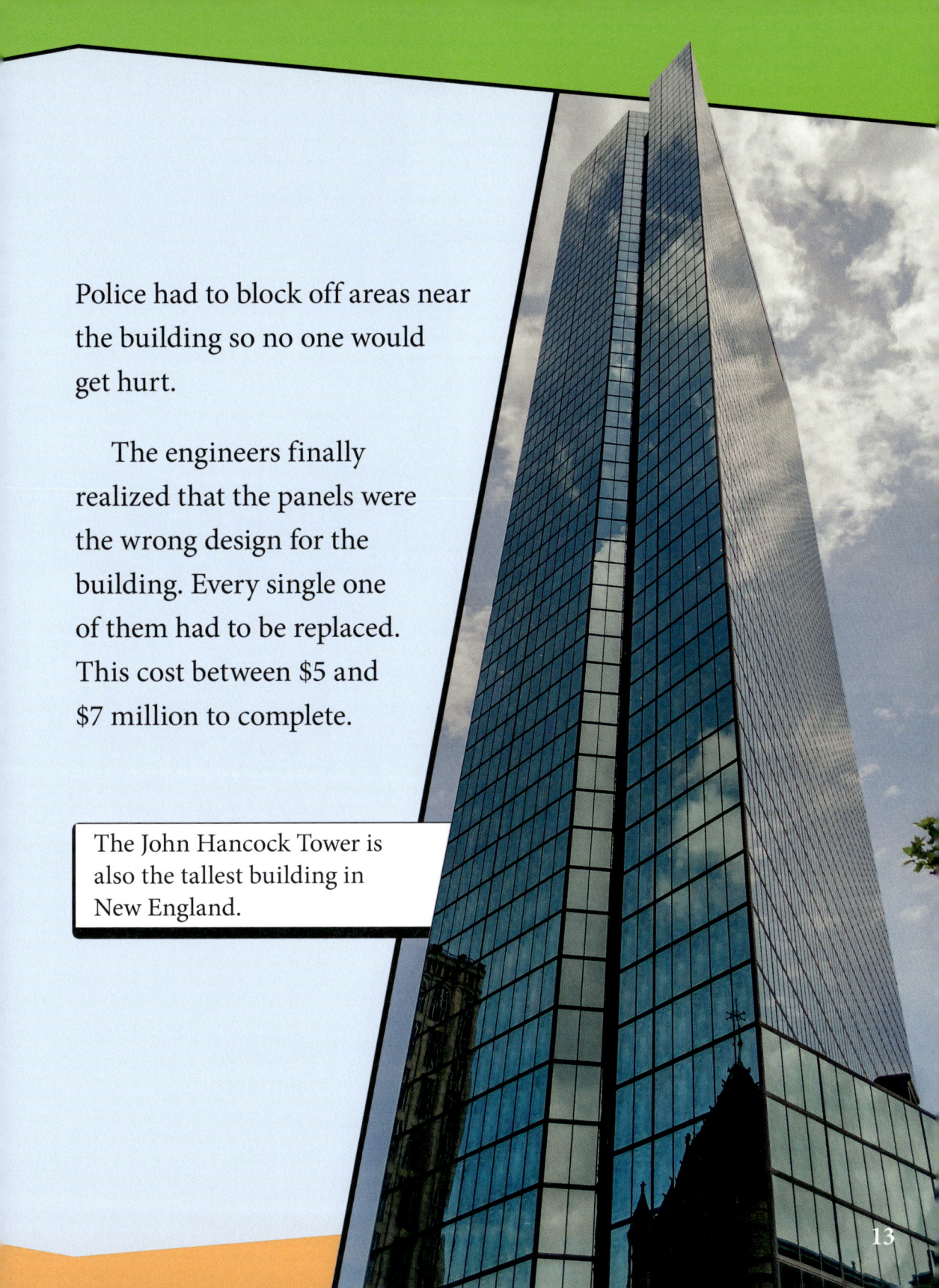

Police had to block off areas near the building so no one would get hurt.

The engineers finally realized that the panels were the wrong design for the building. Every single one of them had to be replaced. This cost between $5 and $7 million to complete.

The John Hancock Tower is also the tallest building in New England.

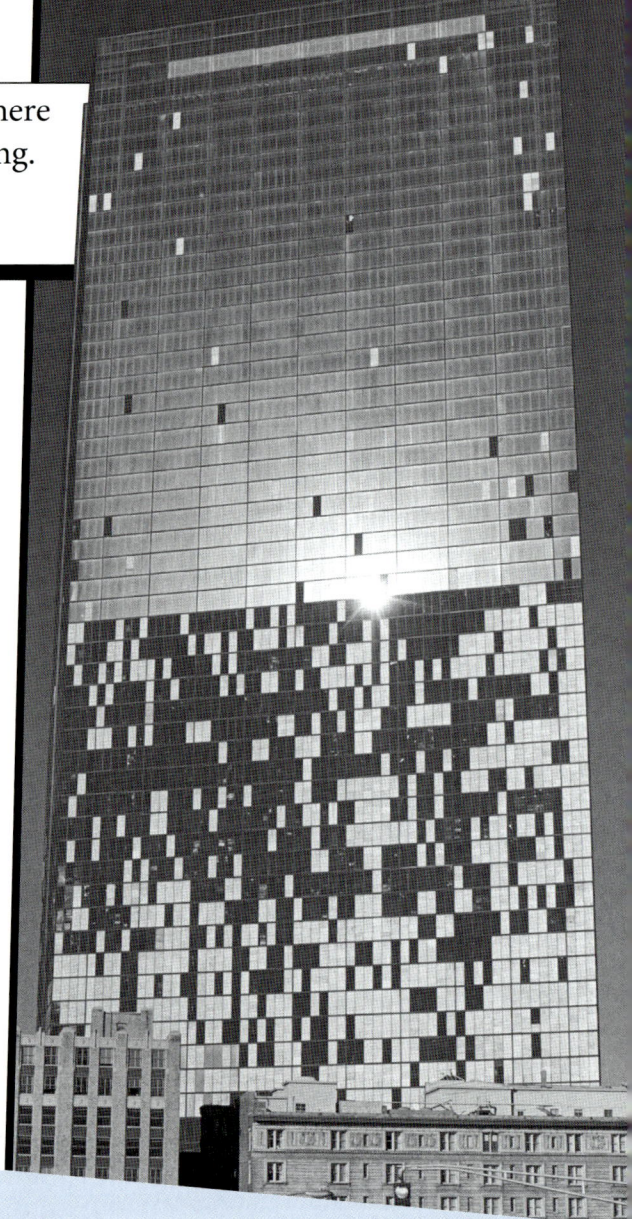

Plywood was used to cover areas where windows had popped off the building. Some people called the tower the Plywood Palace.

Blowing glass wasn't the only problem caused by the wind. Severe storms caused the tower to sway back and forth. Sometimes it even felt like the building was twisting in the wind. People on the upper floors started feeling dizzy, woozy, and seasick.

To correct the problem, the engineers installed a Tuned Mass Damper (TMD).

Tiny Tests

Engineers made models of the Hancock Tower. They placed them inside the Wright Brothers Wind Tunnel at the Massachusetts Institute of Technology (MIT). The model tests helped them discover why the glass panes were falling off. Today wind tunnel tests are done all of the time before skyscrapers are constructed.

TMDs are **pendulum**-like structures that are installed inside things that rock or move.

In the mid-1970s, two TMDs were installed inside the Hancock Tower at opposite ends of the 58th story. The **kinetic energy** from the wind is transferred immediately from the building to the TMDs. The TMDs swoosh back and forth until there is no more kinetic energy left. They reduce the amount of building sway by 40 to 50 percent. Installing them cost an additional $3 million.

FACT: TMDs are used on things like ships, bridges, and communication spires. The Hancock Tower was the first building to have them.

Lessons Learned

Everyday factors, like strong wind, may have no effect on small structures. But the taller the building, the greater the wind force. As wind force increases, the building may bend and sway more, affecting both the inside and the outside of the structure.

CHAPTER 4
THE DEATH RAY
VDARA HOTEL AND SPA

Las Vegas, Nevada

The Vdara Hotel and Spa is located in the center of the Las Vegas Strip. Visitors come to experience entertainment, spa treatments, and even robots who fetch snacks. But the hotel is also known as the Death Ray.

Opened in 2009, the hotel is unique. The glass exterior of the 57-story building is curved into a **concave** shape. Because of that, the building acts like a giant magnifying glass. When the sun strikes the building at certain times of the day, the building reflects a piercing beam of light. This "death ray" strikes right by the swimming pool. Sunbathers by the pool

FACT: Las Vegas is a hot desert city. Temperatures in the summertime are often well over 100°F (37.8°C).

The Vdara offers tourists a 270-degree view of the Las Vegas Strip.

have experienced temperatures that are sometimes 20 degrees hotter than the surrounding area. Singed hair and burned skin have been reported. Even plastic bags have melted.

The pool is located on the third floor of the hotel.

The Vdara owners have never permanently corrected the problem. It would not be an easy fix. The building's exterior would have to be changed from glass to something else. Or the building's shape would need to be altered. They decided both of those options are far too costly. Instead, they simply installed more umbrellas to protect sunbathers from the powerful effects of the "death ray." Nonreflective film covers the glass. It helps—a little bit.

Lessons Learned

Even though a design looks cool on paper, architects must consider how their building will react with natural elements.

Hot Stuff: The Walkie Talkie Center

The Vdara isn't the only building to have a death ray. The Walkie Talkie Center in London, England, is another glass structure with a concave exterior. The buildings also share the same architect—Rafael Viñoly.

Londoners have nicknamed the building the Walkie Scorchie or the Fryscraper. A newspaper reported that the building has melted car parts, caused paint to blister, and even helped fry an egg on a sidewalk. None of these things are common in gray, cloudy London. They are all caused by the building's design.

The building architect, Rafael Viñoly, said he knew the Walkie Talkie Center would reflect the sun. But he said he didn't think it would be such a problem. He claimed there were no tools or software to help him predict just how strong the reflection would be.

CHAPTER 5
ALL ANGLES
RAY AND MARIA STATA CENTER AT MIT

Cambridge, Massachusetts

One look at the Ray and Maria Stata Center and you feel like you're looking at something from the pages of a cartoon. It's original and fun—but fun doesn't always work in the real world.

Completed in 2004, this building is located at the Massachusetts Institute of Technology (MIT). It was designed by architect Frank Gehry. He is known for his creative style and unusual designs.

Most buildings are built with **parallel** lines and 90-degree angles. The Stata Center is different. Some walls are curved. Others are built with sharp, narrow 30-degree angles. The layout inside the Stata Center is just as wild. Some people need to use global positioning systems (GPS) to find their way around.

Getting lost in this piece of artwork was just one problem. The building leaked whenever it rained. The rain caused mold to grow, even outdoors. In the winter, snow and ice would tumble from the roof and block exits. The walls began to crack and break due to stress caused by the building's unusual angles.

The Stata Center covers 720,000 square feet (66,890 square meters). It holds offices, classrooms, a lecture hall, a cafeteria, a fitness center, a childcare center, and other student spaces.

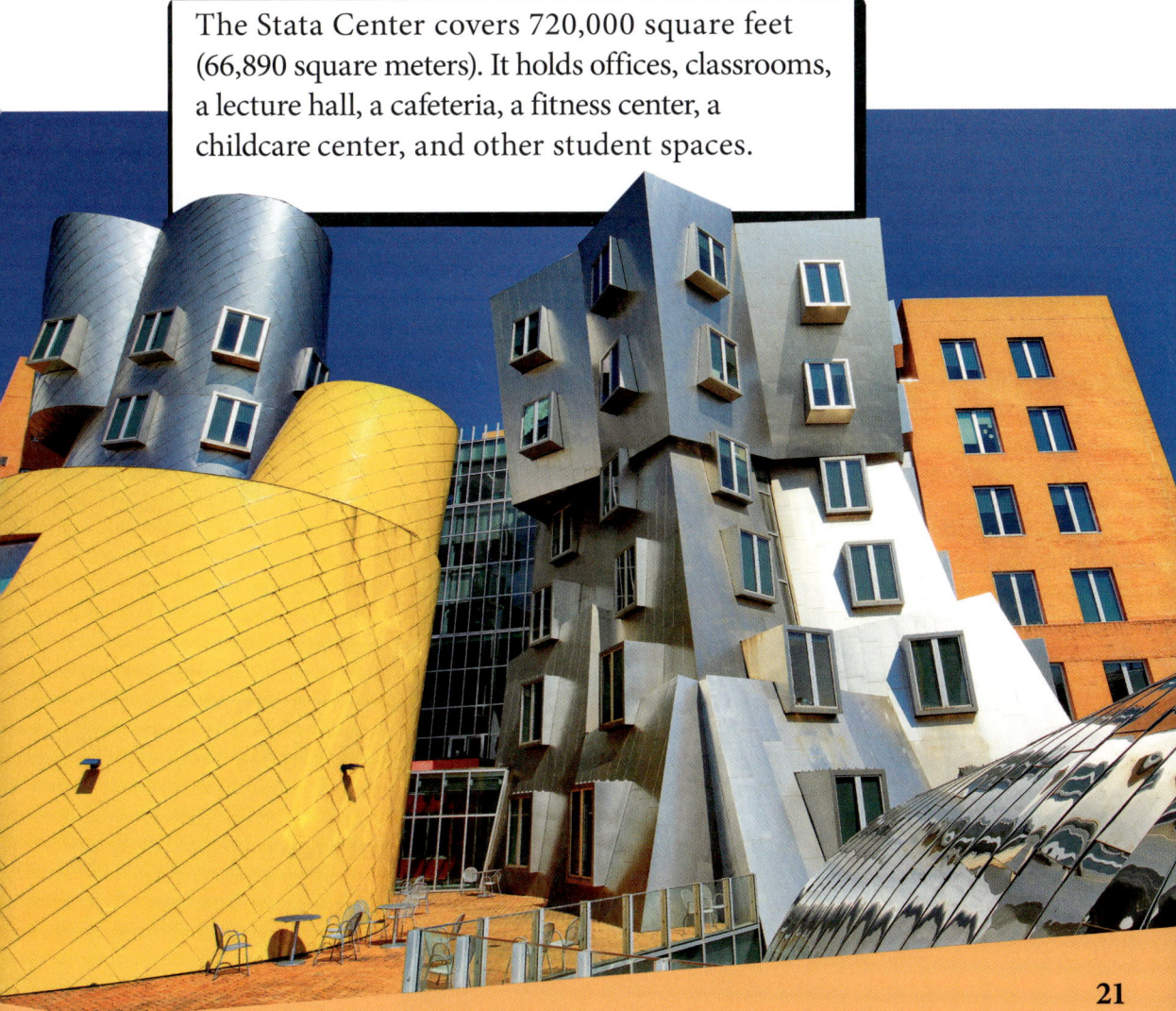

MIT hoped that Gehry's creative mind would encourage the next generation of architects.

IT'S ALL FUN AND GAMES UNTIL . . .

Unfortunately, MIT was left with a big problem on its hands. It cost $300 million to build the center the first time. The school had to pay more for repairs. One section alone cost more than $1.5 million to fix.

In 2007, MIT sued the **architect** and contractors for those design defects.

In response, Gehry blamed MIT for trying to cut costs during construction. Some building elements were left out to save money. He also said that there were many people who worked on the project, and many pieces that had to come together. Both the design and the construction could be at fault.

Experimental Architecture

Frank Gehry has pushed the limit with his designs in many other buildings around the world. These designs include The Dancing House in Prague in the Czech Republic; the Walt Disney Concert Hall in Los Angeles, California; the Experience Music Project Museum in Seattle, Washington; and the Biomuseo in Panama City, Panama.

Lessons Learned

Buildings can have unique, artistic designs. But they must also be practical and functional in the real world. Architects and engineers need to work together to make sure that unusual ideas will actually work out.

CHAPTER 6
BEND AND SNAP
THE AON CENTER

Chicago, Illinois

When it was built in 1974, the Aon Center, formerly known as the Standard Oil Building, and then the Amoco Building, was the fourth-tallest building in the world. It has 83 floors and reaches a height of 1,189 feet (362 m).

The outside of the building was covered in thin rectangles of stone called Carrara marble. The stone was from Italy's Carrara Mountains. The smooth, creamy marble is one of the most expensive marbles in the world. It has been used for famous sculptures and at famous locations, such as Michelangelo's *David* and the lobby of the World Trade Center.

It took 43,000 pounds (19,500 kilograms) of marble to cover the Aon Center. Each panel weighed 275 pounds (124 kg.) The building gleamed white in the sun.

SLIP, SLIDING AWAY

However, even though the stone was great for sculptures, it wasn't terrific to put on skyscrapers. The marble didn't hold up well in the extreme temperature changes that Chicago experiences between winter and summer. The stone pieces would expand on hot days or contract on cold ones. This caused them to **bow**. The stone was also bolted in place. This meant there wasn't any extra room as the stone changed shape. Because of this, some pieces cracked.

As of 2019, the Aon Center is the 22nd-tallest building in the United States.

25

Since the pieces were no longer flat, there were fewer contact points to keep them attached. One piece slid right off and crashed through the roof of a building next door.

STEEL BELTS

After the first piece fell, the building's owners tried to find a way to keep it from happening again. They decided to wrap the building in steel straps, to hold the marble in place. But over the next decade, the stone continued to break. It was feared that more pieces could eventually fall off.

REFACING

In 1989, the owners decided to remove all of the marble. It was

First Canadian Place in Toronto, Canada, had its marble exterior (bottom) replaced with glass and ceramic panels (top) in 2011. It cost $100 million to replace the 45,000 marble sheets.

replaced with thicker pieces of granite. This stone was more durable. It was less affected by nature too. Unfortunately, there was no use for the marble. By that time, it was too warped and weak for anything other than being ground up for construction material.

It cost more than $80 million to reface the building. This was a huge price to pay. The Aon Center had cost less than $120 million to build the first time.

Lessons Learned

First Canadian Place in Toronto, Canada; the Finlandia Hall in Helsinki, Finland; and the Metropolitan in Rochester, New York, are also covered with Carrara marble. All the buildings were constructed around the same time. All had similar disasters. Due to these failures, it is now known that there are certain types of materials that can be used on skyscrapers and certain types that cannot.

CHAPTER 7
LIKE DOMINOES
LOTUS RIVERSIDE

Shanghai, China

The Lotus Riverside was part of a large apartment complex built in 2009. In all, there were 11 buildings. Every building was 13 stories tall, with 629 apartments each.

The complex was nearly complete. But at 5:40 a.m. on June 27, there was a loud noise followed by a cloud of smoke. One of the apartment buildings, Block 7, had toppled over. A reporter for National Public Radio (NPR) said

FACT: Shanghai has grown around 10 percent a year for the past 20 years. Today, more than 24 million people call the city home. That is more than double the population in 1987.

that it looked like "a giant nudged the building over with a fingertip."

One worker, who had been inside to grab his tools, was killed. Luckily, no one else was nearby at that time of the day. The structures were just far enough apart that the fall didn't affect any of the other 10 structures.

After the collapse, the building was righted and reinspected.

During the time of the collapse, construction in China was being done quickly and cheaply. The average life span of a building was only around 30 years.

AND THEY ALL DIDN'T FALL DOWN . . .

The other buildings in the complex did not fall. They were built in the exact same way as Block 7. What happened?

To find out the answer, investigators looked over the scene. They found that construction workers were digging an underground garage next to the south side of Block 7. They had also piled 32 feet (10 m) of soil on the north side. The 3,000 pounds (1,3601 kg) of soil was pressing the building toward a 15-foot (4.6-m)-deep hole. Eventually the soil pushed the building off its foundation, and it toppled over.

FACT: Nearly 500 apartments in the complex had already been sold before the collapse. Some buyers had spent their life savings. Many demanded a refund. Between construction and payouts to buyers, the disaster cost more than 20 million yuan (around $3 million).

Lessons Learned

Before doing any renovation work, it's important to think about how it will affect the foundation of any nearby buildings. Will there still be enough support underneath?

CHAPTER 8
ON DISPLAY
THE CRYSTAL PALACE

London, England

England's Prince Albert dreamed of holding an international exhibition. Inventors could come together for a Great Exhibition of their inventions.

The building the prince imagined would be huge. There would be more than 8 miles (13 km) of display space stretching across Hyde Park. It was the largest building ever constructed. It was also unusually cheap considering its size, with a bill of $186,130 (150,000 British pounds), or $18.6 million (15 million British pounds) today. All the building materials were of British origin.

Around 14,000 exhibitors and 6 million visitors showed up to the Great Exhibition in the Crystal Palace in 1851. Modern marvels were demonstrated, including printing machines, steam engines, folding pianos, early versions of bicycles, and 3-dimensional ink for the blind.

It took nine months to build the iron and glass Crystal Palace.

FACT: The Crystal Palace was made of **prefabricated** parts that were brought to Hyde Park. They were put together there. Although this is a common building method now, at the time it was new and unusual.

After the exhibition was over, the structure was rebuilt at Penge Common in London. It opened to the public in 1854. More than 2 million people visited the palace every year. With entertainment, sporting events, gardens, and roller coaster and hot air balloon rides, it was the world's first theme park.

HOT IRON

Some critics noted that cast iron, which was used to build the Palace, could be brittle. That meant that it could collapse or buckle suddenly, and without warning. Several iron bridges had recently collapsed, and people worried that wind or vibration would topple the Palace. Engineers had designed tests to show how stable the iron pieces used for the building could be.

No one thought the Crystal Palace would be a fire risk. They were wrong.

On November 30, 1936, a fire started inside the building. **Flammable** materials, including the old wooden floors, burned quickly. A huge 4,500-pipe organ, once a marvel on display, drew air directly into the Palace and fed the fire.

Thousands of people gathered to watch the blaze. Nearly 90 fire engines and more than 430 firefighters showed up to help. But they couldn't save the Crystal Palace. Fortunately, no lives were lost.

Lessons Learned

This was the first time private engineers had tested building materials for safety. During the stability tests, the iron showed itself to be strong. But under high temperatures, iron loses its ability to support a lot of weight. The builders never considered fire to be a threat. During the fire, the iron beams bent and collapsed. It's important to take all risks into consideration when building.

The cause of the fire has never been discovered. But some experts think old wiring or a carelessly thrown cigarette could be to blame.

CHAPTER 9
NO GOAL
GROLSCH VESTE

Enschede, Netherlands

The Grolsch Veste was originally built in 1997. The stadium, home to the soccer team FC Twente, was expanded in 2011. It was the second stage in the stadium's expansion. Once finished, 30,000 fans would fill the seats.

A few weeks before it was supposed to be finished, the roof suddenly fell. Two **girders** buckled, killing two people and injuring at least nine more. According to an article by the BBC, a witness said that "it collapsed with a huge noise like a house of cards."

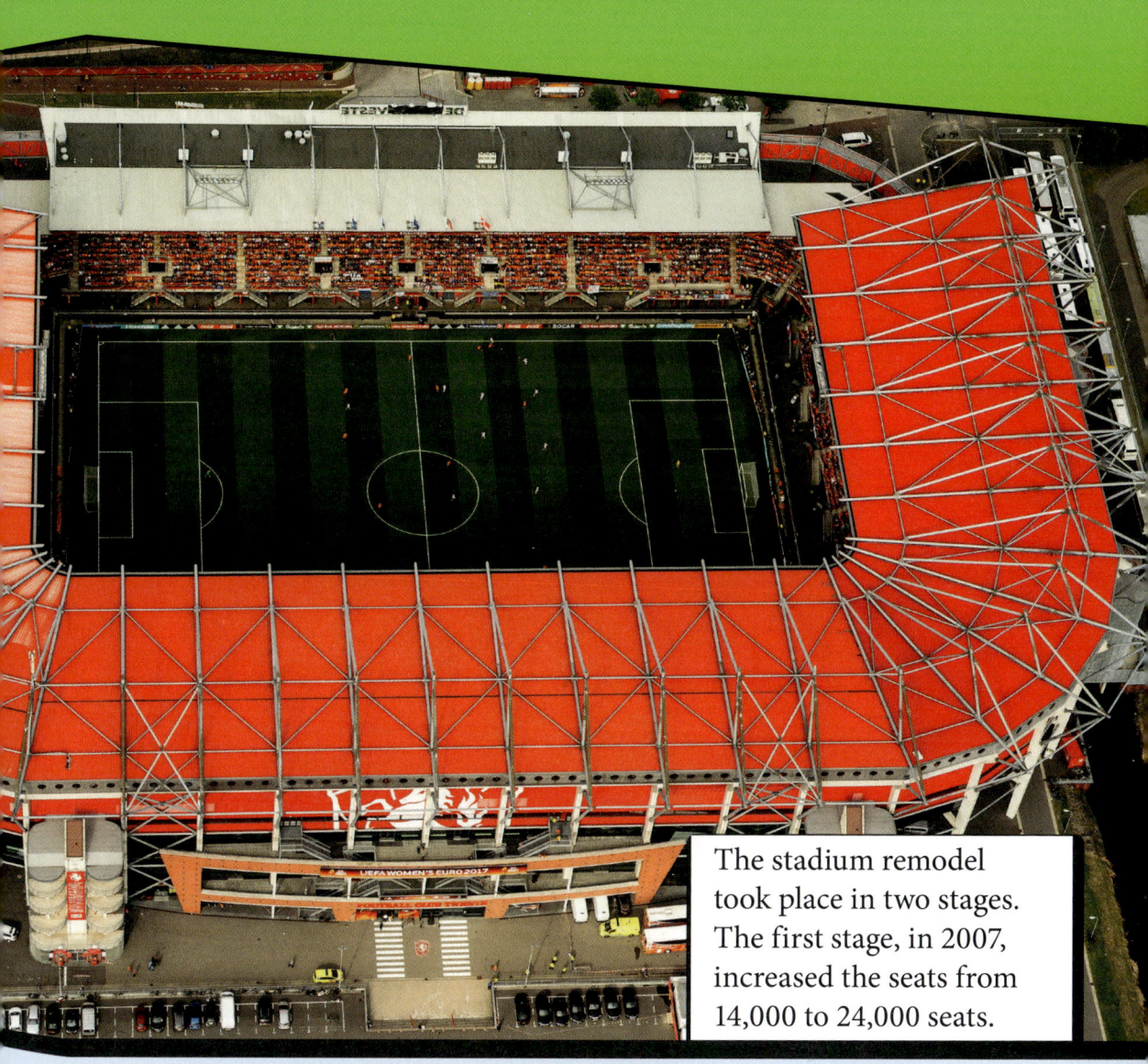

The stadium remodel took place in two stages. The first stage, in 2007, increased the seats from 14,000 to 24,000 seats.

Another Stadium Failure

Fidenae Amphitheater was built in AD 27 in Rome, Italy. It was built quickly and inexpensively in order to host an upcoming gladiator game. Because of its cheap construction, the structure collapsed during the event. Records vary, but between 20,000 and 50,000 people are said to have died. After this disaster, the Roman government said that all future amphitheaters had to be inspected for safety.

an exterior view of the stadium collapse

Investigations after the collapse showed that the contractor did not pay attention to how the roof was being put together. Some **lateral** bracing had not been added yet. In some places, that meant that there wasn't enough bracing to hold up the roof. A roof won't stay up if it doesn't have the right amount of support in the right places.

Why Did It Happen?

Why didn't someone catch this error before the roof collapsed? Usually there are safety checks and building inspections. But there wasn't on this job. The main contractor did not assign anyone to do the safety checks. This mistake led to the disaster.

Lessons Learned

Safety checks and building inspections are necessary on every job. They prevent collapses, fires, and other structural problems in a building. They protect both the building and the workers. They also protect people who later might use the buildings.

Many small issues can add up and lead to one big issue. Even if the design looks great on a computer, computers (or engineers) can make mistakes. Sometimes materials are damaged on the way to the building site. Other times those materials aren't maintained once the building is complete. Construction requires a lot of small pieces working together.

CHAPTER 10
NOT-SO-MIGHTY MALL
SAMPOONG DEPARTMENT STORE

Seoul, South Korea

The Sampoong department store was built in 1989. With more than 550 stores, the bright pink building was a busy shopping site—until it collapsed in 1995.

There were a number of problems with the building from the very beginning.

It was built on the site of a former garbage dump. Small structures could work on such unstable ground, but large structures need a firm base. The shopping center had a total of nine floors—four floors underground and five aboveground. The original contractor was fired when he questioned the safety of adding the fifth floor.

The space was originally meant for apartments. It was later supposed to become offices. That meant that far fewer people would have been in the structure at any given time. But as a department store, about

40,000 people visited every day. This added to the load that the building's foundation had to carry.

In order to get safety and building inspections passed, the building's owner **bribed** government officials. That way he could build whatever he wanted however he wanted. He saved money by using cheap concrete. He also reduced the number of steel reinforcements in the framework.

The Sampoong department store opened on July 7, 1990.

FATEFUL DAY

The store executives knew that there were problems with the building. On June 27, 1995, water from the fifth-floor pool started leaking into other floors. There were big cracks in many of the walls. A gas leak was reported. Engineers came in and inspected. They said that the building was unsafe. But the building's owner brought in his own workers, who said that everything was fine. They advised repairing the cracks and moving expensive merchandise out of the way, just in case.

The store collapse was the largest nonwartime disaster in South Korean history.

On June 29, big cracks could be seen across the roof. The cracks had been caused by the huge 45-ton (41-metric-ton) air conditioners on top of the building. The owner made the decision not to evacuate the department store, which was unusually busy. The air conditioners fell through the roof later that day, taking out support columns on the way down. More than 500 people were killed, and another 900 were injured.

Lessons Learned

Building codes, inspections, and safety measures must be taken seriously. Building owners should not be allowed to make up their own rules just to save money. The owner of the building and 23 others involved were given jail sentences for their **corruption**.

Humans have always wanted to build. Lessons come from what we learn before, during, and after construction. The more we learn from our mistakes, the more likely it is that we will avoid building blunders. Sometimes the best lessons come from mistakes.

TIMELINE

27 AD: Fidenae Amphitheater
- Cost to build: unknown
- Cost to fix: unknown

1173–1399: Leaning Tower of Pisa
- Cost to build: $4.1 million, modern estimate
- Cost to fix: $27 million (completed in 2001)

1360: Crooked Spire Church
- Cost to build: unknown
- Cost to fix: unknown

1851: The Crystal Palace
- Cost to build: $18.6 million (15 million British pounds), modern estimate
- Cost to fix: unknown

1968: John Hancock Tower
- Cost to build: $75 to $175 million (amounts vary, and costs to fix are likely part of this amount)
- Cost to fix: $5 to 7 million for the windows; $3 million for the TMDs; $11.6 million for damages to a local church

1974: Aon Center
- Cost to build: $120 million
- Cost to fix: $80 million

1989: Sampoong Department Store
- Cost to build: unknown
- Cost to fix: $216 million; in addition, the building owner and 23 others were sentenced to jail and fined. The city of Seoul, Korea, gave up to $257,400 to relatives of the people who had died.

2004: Ray and Maria Stata Center
- Cost to build: $300 million
- Cost to fix: at least $1.5 million

2009: Vdara Hotel
- Cost to build: unknown; part of the CityCenter, which cost $8.5 billion to complete
- Cost to fix: unknown

2009: Lotus Riverside
- Cost to build: unknown
- Cost to fix: $3 million

2011: Grolsch Veste
- Cost to build: $37.6 million (includes original building, plus upgrades in 2008 and 2011)
- Cost to fix: unknown; the building and construction firms paid fines of about $56,000 and another $84,000 toward a victim support fund

GLOSSARY

architect (AR-ki-tekt)—a person who designs buildings and advises in their construction

bow (BOH)—to bend in a curve or an arc

bracing (BRAY-sing)—interior supports that help hold up a structure

bribe (BRIBE)—giving money or gifts to persuade someone to do something, especially something illegal or dishonest

concave (kahn-KAYV)—hollow and curved, like the inside of a bowl

corrupt (kuh-RUPT)—willingness to do things that are wrong or illegal to get money, favors, or power

cure (KYOOR)—to prepare building materials, usually through a chemical or physical process

flammable (FLA-muh-buhl)—likely to catch fire

girder (GUHR-duhr)—a horizontal piece that supports vertical pieces in a building

kinetic energy (ki-NET-ik EN-ur-jee)—energy associated with motion

lateral (LAT-ur-uhl)—relating to the sides of an object

parallel (PA-ruh-lel)—to be in a straight line and an equal distance apart

pendulum (PEN-dyoo-luhm)—a weight that swings back and forth

prefabricated (pre-FAB-ruh-kay-tuhd)—premade sections of a building that can be joined together on-site

spire (SPY-uhr)—a tapering pointed structure on the top of a building

stabilize (STAY-buh-lyz)—to make something unlikely to fall

superstitious (soo-pur-STI-shuhs)—an irrational belief that an action can affect the outcome of a future event

superstructure (SOO-per-struhk-shur)—the part of a building that is above the foundation

warp (WORP)—to become bent or twisted

READ MORE

Newland, Sonya. *Extraordinary Skyscrapers: The Science of How and Why They Were Built*. North Mankato, MN: Capstone Press, 2019.

Noyce, Pendred E. *Engineering Bridges: Connecting the World*. Boston: Tumblehome Learning, Inc., 2019.

Rusch, Elizabeth. *The Big One: The Cascadia Earthquakes and the Science of Saving Lives*. Boston: HMH Books for Young Readers, Harcourt, 2020.

INTERNET SITES

Architecture for Kids
http://archkidecture.org/

Engineering for Kids
https://www.engineeringforkids.com/

Easy Science for Kids (Bridge Building)
https://easyscienceforkids.com/all-about-bridges/

Kid-Friendly Construction Projects
https://www.popularmechanics.com/home/how-to/g22/10-diy-toys-you-can-build-with-your-kids/

INDEX

Aon Center, 24–27

bracing, 10, 11, 38

collapses, 6, 28–29, 30–31, 34, 36, 38, 39, 42, 43
Crooked Spire Church, 8–11
Crystal Palace, 32–35
curved buildings, 16, 19, 20
cutting costs, 23, 30, 32, 37, 41

Fidenae Amphitheater, 37
fires, 34, 35, 39
First Canadian Place, 26

Gehry, Frank, 20, 22, 23
girders, 36
Great Exhibition, 32–33
green wood, 10, 11
Grolsch Veste, 36–39

heavy weights, 10

inspections, 37, 39, 41, 42, 43

John Hancock Tower, 12–15

Leaning Tower of Pisa, 4–7
Lotus Riverside, 28–31

Massachusetts Institute of Technology (MIT), 14, 20–23

panels, 12, 13, 14, 24, 25, 26, 27
prefabricated parts, 33

Ray and Maria Stata Center, 20–23
reflections, 12, 16, 18

Sampoong Department Store, 40–43
skyscrapers, 12, 14, 25, 27
St. Mary and All Saints Church. *See* Crooked Spire Church
swaying, 14, 15

testing, 14, 35
Tuned Mass Damper (TMD), 14–15

Vdara Hotel and Spa, 16–19
Viñoly, Rafael, 19

Walkie Talkie Center, 19
weather, 12, 14, 15, 16, 17, 19, 21, 25